STUDY GUIDE

Blessing and Praise

Benedictions and Doxologies in Scripture

H.B. Charles Jr.

LIGONIER MINISTRIES
Renew your Mind.
LIGONIER.ORG | 800-435-4343

421 Ligonier Court, Sanford, FL 32771
Email: info@ligonier.org

Printed in China.

Contents

Introduction

The Bible contains numerous blessings from God and praises to God. These summary statements of blessing and praise are full of rich theological truths for your edification and nourishment. In *Blessing and Praise,* Dr. H.B. Charles Jr. draws out these truths in short expositions of some of the most instructive benedictions and doxologies in Scripture. Surveying the content of each pronouncement of blessing and praise, he explains how they ought to affect our worship and daily walk with God.

This study guide is a companion to the video teaching series. Whether you are using the DVDs, streaming the videos on Ligonier.org, or going through the course in Ligonier Connect, this resource is designed to help you make the most of the learning experience. For each message in the series, there is a corresponding lesson in this guide. Here is what you will find in each lesson:

INTRODUCTION	The introduction is a brief paragraph that summarizes the content covered in the lecture and considered in the study guide lesson. **How to use:** Use the introduction to each lesson to get a sense of the big picture before watching the video. Refer to these statements as you work through the study guide to remind you of what you have already covered and where you are headed.
LEARNING GOALS	The learning goals are the knowledge and skills that the study guide lesson will endeavor to equip you with as you work through the lecture content. **How to use:** Familiarize yourself with the goals of each lesson before engaging with its contents. Keeping the overall purpose in mind as you watch each video and reflect on or discuss the questions will help you get the most out of each lesson.
KEY IDEAS	The key ideas are the major points or takeaways from the lecture. **How to use:** Use these ideas to prepare yourself for each lesson and to review previous lessons. They describe specifically the knowledge that each lecture is communicating.

REFLECTION & DISCUSSION QUESTIONS	The questions are the guided reflection and/or discussion component of the lesson that are intended to help you prepare for, process, and organize what you are learning. **How to use:** Reflect on individually or discuss in a group the questions in the order in which they appear in the lesson. The time stamps in the right margin indicate where the answers to questions during the video can be found.
PRAYER	The prayer section offers suggestions for how to close the lesson in prayer with respect to what was taught in the lecture. **How to use:** Consider using each lesson's prayer section as a guide to personal or group prayer. These sections follow the ACTS prayer model, which you can learn more about in R.C. Sproul's Crucial Questions booklet *Does Prayer Change Things?* This helpful guide is available as a free e-book at Ligonier.org.
REVIEW QUIZ	The review quiz is a set of six multiple-choice questions that appears at the end of each lesson. **How to use:** Use each quiz to check your comprehension and memory of the major points covered in each lecture. It will be most beneficial to your learning if you take a lesson's quiz either sometime between lessons or just before you begin the next lesson in the study guide.
ANSWER KEY	The answer key provides explanations for the reflection and discussion questions and answers to the multiple-choice questions in the review quiz. **How to use:** Use the answer key to check your own answers or when you do not know the answer. Note: Do not give in too quickly; struggling for a few moments to recall an answer reinforces it in your mind.

Study Schedules

The following table suggests four plans for working through the *Blessing and Praise* video teaching series and this companion study guide. Whether you are going through this series on your own or with a group, these schedules should help you plan your study path.

	Extended 10-Week Plan	Standard 8-Week Plan	Abbreviated 6-Week Plan	Intensive 4-Week Plan
Week	**Lesson**			
1	*	1	1	1 & 2
2	1	2	2 & 3	3 & 4
3	2	3	4	5 & 6
4	3	4	5	7 & 8
5	4	5	6 & 7	
6	5	6	8	
7	6	7		
8	7	8		
9	8			
10	*			

* For these weeks, rather than completing lessons, spend your time discussing and praying about your learning goals for the study (the first week) and the most valuable takeaways from the study (the last week).

1

The Ability of God

INTRODUCTION

Christians long to be assured that God hears them and is able to meet their deepest needs when they pray. Yet many of us do not rightly understand what prayer is or how we ought to pray. In this introductory lesson, Dr. Charles explains the importance of learning to pray in light of the power and glory of God in the Apostle Paul's doxology in Ephesians 3:20–21.

LEARNING GOALS

When you have finished this lesson, you should be able to:

- Identify doxologies in Scripture
- Recognize the God-centered nature of Paul's prayer in Ephesians 3:14–21
- Know that the purpose of prayer is to glorify God

KEY IDEAS

- We best learn how to pray by studying the God who answers prayer.
- God is able to do far more than we could ask or think because He is infinitely powerful and omniscient.
- God is glorified in the church and in Christ, whenever He works His power within us.

REFLECTION & DISCUSSION QUESTIONS

Before the Video

What Do You Think?

Take a moment to answer the following questions. They will prepare you for the lecture.

- Why are you interested in participating in a study on benedictions and doxologies?

- Why is it important for you to learn to pray in a God-glorifying way? Are there areas in which you would like to grow in your prayer life?

Scripture Reading

Now to him who is able to do far more abundantly than all that we ask or think, according to the power at work within us, to him be glory in the church and in Christ Jesus throughout all generations, forever and ever. Amen.

—Ephesians 3:20–21

- What does this passage reveal about God's ability to answer our prayers?

During the Video

Answer the following questions while you watch the video. They will guide you through the lecture.

Able to Answer *0:00–17:26*

- What is the best way to learn how to pray?

- What can we learn from the structure of the prayer in Ephesians 3:14–21?

- How does God work His power within us?

Worthy of Praise *17:26–26:24*

- What ought to be the purpose of all our prayers?

- What are the two platforms on which God is glorified?

After the Video

Answer the following questions after you have finished the lecture. They will help you identify and summarize the major points.

- "Sometimes we short-circuit our own prayers because we say 'Amen' too soon." Why did Dr. Charles make this assertion?

  If you are in a group, encourage the members to discuss the content of their prayers. Consider questions like this: How should we bring our prayers to a close after we have brought our personal requests to God?

- In this lesson, a distinction was made between God's working "according to" His power and God's working "out of" His power. What is significant about this distinction?

  If you are in a group, discuss the ways in which we think about God's power to meet our needs. Consider questions like these: Do you ever feel as though your needs and burdens are so great that there is no hope? Have you been in a situation in which you were overwhelmed by a certain need, only to experience God's powerful work to do more than what you asked or imagined He could do?

- Why should we not worry when we do not "feel" God's power in us? What does Scripture teach us about God's power and our weakness?

  If you are in a group, have the members discuss how God has used their sense of weakness to drive them to Him in prayer. Encourage them to talk about times in which they have recognized God's power at work in them when they did not "feel" His power at work.

PRAYER

Commit what you have learned from God's Word in this lesson to prayer.

- Praise God for manifesting His power in your life in answer to your prayers.
- Confess how often you forget that the purpose of prayer is to bring glory to God.

- Thank God for being aware of your needs, even when you are unaware of them.
- Ask God to enable you to rely more fully on His power to meet your deepest needs.

REVIEW QUIZ

Use these multiple-choice questions to measure what you learned from this lesson.

1. Why did Donald Grey Barnhouse once tell his congregation, "Prayer changes nothing"?
   a. God has already determined what He will do in your life.
   b. God, not prayer, changes things.
   c. God doesn't do what we ask.
   d. God has made us free.

2. What makes all prayer effective?
   a. Sincerity
   b. Boldness
   c. Articulation
   d. God-centeredness

3. How does God's power work in us?
   a. Through the church
   b. Through our studying prayer
   c. Through the indwelling of the Holy Spirit
   d. Through His making us feel His power

4. What is the ultimate purpose of all true prayer?
   a. To increase our faith
   b. To give us peace
   c. To make us humble
   d. To bring glory to God

5. What was articulated in this lesson as impossible to have a low view of if you have a high view of Christ?
   a. The church
   b. Yourself
   c. Other people
   d. All of the above

6. What does the word *amen* mean?
   a. "We hope so"
   b. "The end"
   c. "So be it"
   d. "To God be the glory"

Answer Key—The Ability of God

REFLECTION & DISCUSSION QUESTIONS

Before the Video

What Do You Think?

These are personal questions. The answers should be based on your own knowledge and experience.

Scripture Reading

- What does this passage reveal about God's ability to answer our prayers?

  This passage teaches us that God is infinitely powerful and omniscient and is therefore able to meet our deepest needs—even beyond all that we could ask or think. It reveals that God works His power in His people for His own glory. The God who powerfully answers prayers is the God who is glorified in the church and in Christ.

During the Video

Able to Answer

- What is the best way to learn how to pray?

  We do not best learn how to pray by undertaking a study of prayer; we best learn how to pray by studying the prayer-answering God to whom we pray. Prayer works because the sovereign power of God works in answer to our prayers. As we grow in our knowledge of God, we learn to pray to Him as we ought. As Dr. Charles explained, "Christian living must always flow from Christian truth."

- What can we learn from the structure of the prayer in Ephesians 3:14–21?

  The structure of the prayer highlights the fact that all effective prayer is centered on God. Both before and after the Apostle's petitions are two great statements about God—namely, He is "the Father, from whom every family in heaven and on earth is named," and He "is able to do far more abundantly than all that we ask or think."

- How does God work His power within us?

  God is infinite in power and is therefore Himself *the power. God comes and dwells in His people by the Holy Spirit. The power that God works in us is brought about by the indwelling of the Spirit. Though we are, in and of ourselves, weak people, God works His power in us to resist temptation, live obediently, serve faithfully, witness boldly, and suffer joyfully.*

Worthy of Praise

- What ought to be the purpose of all our prayers?

  Paul closes his prayer with the words "to him be glory." Accordingly, the purpose of all prayer is the glory of God. As Dr. Charles stated, "The God who is able to answer your biggest request is the God who is worthy to receive your highest praise." We must learn to pray for things that would bring glory to God and to praise Him when He has met our needs by His powerful work within us.

- What are the two platforms on which God is glorified?

  God is glorified in the church and in Christ. Ephesians 3:20–21 is the only doxology in the New Testament that contains a reference to the church. When the people of God pray for things that bring glory to God—and God answers those prayers—the church glorifies God by praising Him. The glory of God is displayed in Christ. Jesus is the glory of God. We see the glory of God fully displayed only "in the face of Jesus Christ" (2 Cor. 4:6).

After the Video

- "Sometimes we short-circuit our own prayers because we say 'Amen' too soon." Why did Dr. Charles make this assertion?

  We often end our prayers before we have praised the God who is able to answer our prayers above all that we could ask or think. We tend to bring a list of our requests to God without recognizing that God wants us to pray to Him so that He would receive all the glory.

- In this lesson, a distinction was made between God's working "according to" His power and God's working "out of" His power. What is significant about this distinction?

  God doesn't have power out of which He works. He is infinitely powerful. He is all-powerful. God works "according to" His own infinite power in the lives of His people. This distinction is crucial when we come to God with our needs. The ability of God to surpass our requests and perceived needs is limitless.

- Why should we not worry when we do not "feel" God's power in us? What does Scripture teach us about God's power and our weakness?

  We frequently get discouraged because we do not feel the power of God at work in us. Instead, we should be encouraged to come to God when we feel weak, because we are weak. It is in time of weakness that God works His almighty power in us. The Apostle Paul pleaded with the Lord to take away his debilitating weakness. Rather than doing so, the Lord responded, "My grace is sufficient for you, for my power is made perfect in weakness" (2 Cor. 12:9).

REVIEW QUIZ

Lesson 1

1. **B.**
To emphasize the point that God, rather than prayer, has the power to effect change, Donald Grey Barnhouse once told his congregation, "Prayer changes nothing." Dr. Charles explained, "Prayer works not because of the words we say, the promises we claim, or the faith we demonstrate. Prayer works because of the sovereign power, the omnipotent power, of almighty God."

2. **D.**
All effective prayer is God-centered prayer. When we acknowledge who God is and that He is able to hear and answer far beyond what we ask or think according to His power and knowledge, we will be able to pray as we ought to pray.

3. **C.**
God works His power in us by the Holy Spirit. God is infinite in power. When He comes to dwell in the hearts of His people by the Holy Spirit, He works His power within them. As Dr. Charles explained, when someone believes in Christ for salvation, the Holy Spirit takes up residence in his or her heart "immediately, permanently, completely."

4. **D.**
The ultimate purpose of all true prayer is to bring glory to God. God doesn't answer prayer, first and foremost, because of us. He does so in order to receive glory in the church and in Christ.

5. **A.**
In this lesson, an emphasis was placed on having a high view of the church. The church is the platform by which God is glorified, so we cannot have a low view of the church if we have a high view of Christ. Christ is the Bridegroom of the church, and the church is the bride of Christ. He is the Shepherd of His sheep and Head of His church.

6. **C.**
The word amen *means "so be it." We conclude our prayers with this word because we are expressing our confidence that God is able to do all that He has promised to do and that He will do it for His own glory. It is not an uncertain well-wishing. It is not a word simply expressing hope. It is a confident affirmation that God answers prayers.*

2

Equipped by God

INTRODUCTION

Benedictions are pronouncements of God's blessing, founded on truths about God. With each benediction, God is declaring His intention to bless His people, and He is indicating the specific way in which He will bring that blessing about in their lives. In this lesson, Dr. Charles unfolds the teaching of Hebrews 13:20–21 concerning what God has done for us in Christ and what He promises to do for us in Christ.

LEARNING GOALS

When you have finished this lesson, you should be able to:

- Explain the purpose of a benediction
- Identify the historical context of the benediction in Hebrews 13:20–21
- Define the word *peace* as it is used in Hebrews 13:20–21
- Understand what this benediction means when it speaks of being equipped by God
- Know what it means to do God's will

KEY IDEAS

- God is intent to make His help, strength, and power available to His people in Christ.
- What God has done for us through the death and resurrection of Christ is the foundation of His continued blessing in our lives.
- In Christ, God equips and enables His people to do His will.

REFLECTION & DISCUSSION QUESTIONS

Before the Video

What Do You Think?

Take a moment to answer the following questions. They will prepare you for the lecture.

- Have you ever been to a church in which the pastor pronounced a benediction at the end of the worship service? If so, what were your thoughts about that part of the service?

- In what ways do you think about connecting Christ's work in the past with His blessing in the future?

Scripture Reading

Now may the God of peace who brought again from the dead our Lord Jesus, the great shepherd of the sheep, by the blood of the eternal covenant, equip you with everything good that you may do his will, working in us that which is pleasing in his sight, through Jesus Christ, to whom be glory forever and ever. Amen.

—Hebrews 13:20–21

- How does God's past work in Christ affect the declaration of the future blessing of His people? What is that future blessing?

During the Video

Answer the following questions while you watch the video. They will guide you through the lecture.

Past Blessing *0:00–15:18*

- What is a benediction?

- How does the benediction in Hebrews 13:20–21 connect God's power to raise Christ to His ability to work in us?

- What issue was the author of Hebrews addressing when he wrote this letter?

- What are two possible interpretations of the phrase "through the blood of the eternal covenant"?

Future Blessing *15:18–24:08*

- What two petitions does the writer make in Hebrews 13:21?

- According to the passage, with what does God equip believers?

- To what end does the writer pray that God would equip His people with every good thing?

After the Video

Answer the following questions after you have finished the lecture. They will help you identify and summarize the major points.

- According to Dr. Charles, this benediction gives us three reasons why we ought to trust God for the help we need. What are those reasons?

  If you are in a group, have the members discuss how these three things affect our Christian life. Encourage the members to talk about how their present needs are met by each of these.

- From where does true peace come? How does John Blanchard define the phrase "the peace of God"?

  If you are in a group, have the members discuss the subject of peace. Consider asking questions like these: How have you defined peace before this study? Have you largely understood it to be the absence of hostility, animosity, and trouble? What did you think about Dr. Charles' suggestion that it is a positive statement of blessing?

- How ought the truth about God's raising Jesus from the dead affect our Christian lives?

If you are in a group, have the members discuss how often they think about the resurrection of Jesus. Consider asking questions like these: How much power do you think it takes to raise someone from the dead? In light of the power at work in the resurrection, how confident should we be that God is able to work whatever power we need in us? Encourage the members to pray that God will work His resurrection power in their lives for their greatest spiritual needs.

PRAYER

Commit what you have learned from God's Word in this lesson to prayer.

- Praise God for what He has done for you through Christ's death and resurrection.
- Confess your lack of dependence on God's resurrection power for your greatest needs.
- Thank God for promising to equip you with every good thing.
- Ask God to increase your faith in Him and in His ability to equip you to do His will.

REVIEW QUIZ

Use these multiple-choice questions to measure what you learned from this lesson.

1. Who said, "God helps those who help themselves"?
   a. Solomon
   b. Saul of Tarsus
   c. Benjamin Franklin
   d. Thomas Jefferson
2. According to Dr. Charles, what aspect of Christ's resurrection do the Epistles emphasize?
   a. The fact of the resurrection
   b. The evidence of the resurrection
   c. The significance of the resurrection
   d. All of the above
3. According to Dr. Charles, what is biblical peace?
   a. The end of trouble
   b. The absence of hostility
   c. Wholeness and fulfillment
   d. Freedom from anxiety and worry

4. Which special office does the writer of Hebrews focus on when he speaks of Jesus' exaltation and present intercessory ministry for believers?
   a. Prophet
   b. Priest
   c. King
   d. Judge

5. Which gifts are included in the reference to "everything good" in this benediction?
   a. Love, joy, peace
   b. Miraculous healing
   c. Prophecy, tongues, knowledge
   d. Ruling, teaching, administration

6. What does the writer of Hebrews mean when he speaks of believers' doing God's will?
   a. Discovering what God wants of you
   b. Accomplishing what God desires of you in your own strength
   c. Doing what is pleasing to God, by the working of His power in you
   d. Waiting for God to act in your life

Answer Key—Equipped by God

REFLECTION & DISCUSSION QUESTIONS

Before the Video

What Do You Think?

These are personal questions. The answers should be based on your own knowledge and experience.

Scripture Reading

- How does God's past work in Christ affect the declaration of the future blessing of His people? What is that future blessing?

  Since God has raised Jesus from the dead, He is able to work all the power necessary in us to enable us to do His will. The future blessing is His equipping and empowering us with every good thing to do His will.

During the Video

Past Blessing

- What is a benediction?

  The word benediction *means "blessing." In the lesson, Dr. Charles explains that many pastors prayerfully announce a divine blessing over the people of God at the close of the worship service. Many times, the benediction is simply a pastoral announcement of some divine blessing in Scripture.*

- How does the benediction in Hebrews 13:20–21 connect God's power to raise Christ to His ability to work in us?

  In this benediction, the writer focuses explicitly on the resurrection of Jesus for the first time in the letter. He does so in order to drive home the point that since God raised Jesus from the dead by His infinite power, He is able to help you to be all that He wants you to be. As Dr. Charles stated, "The resurrection of Jesus Christ is the stress test of divine omnipotence, whatever we face."

- What issue was the author of Hebrews addressing when he wrote this letter?

  The Hebrew Christians were tempted to walk away from the faith on account of the persecution they were enduring. The writer is encouraging his readers to continue on in the Christian faith since Christ is infinitely better than what they had in Judaism.

- What are two possible interpretations of the phrase "through the blood of the eternal covenant"?

The phrase could be linked either to God's raising Jesus from the dead or to God's equipping believers with every good thing. If related to the resurrection of Jesus, the idea would be that Jesus' resurrection was proof that His sacrificial death was accepted by His Father. The resurrection happened only because Jesus accomplished redemption through the shedding of His blood. If we understand the phrase to be connected to the latter part of the verse, it would mean that God has secured us through the blood of Christ; therefore, we can trust God to do for us what we are unable to do for ourselves. It is not entirely clear which idea the writer of Hebrews intended. Regardless, both options are plausible.

Future Blessing

- What two petitions does the writer make in Hebrews 13:21?

  In this benediction, there is a prayer for equipping and a prayer for enabling. The writer first prays that God will equip His people, making them ready, prepared, and restored by giving them every good thing. He then prays that God will enable His people to do His will. This means that He will give us what we need so that we have the power to resist temptation, obey, serve, witness, and suffer.

- According to the passage, with what does God equip believers?

  The writer prays that God will equip believers with every good thing. In the lesson, Dr. Charles explained that "everything good" refers to "the comprehensiveness of God's good gifts"—namely, love, joy, peace, goodness, kindness, gentleness, and self-control. There is also a sense in which the writer is saying that God gives us Himself, since He dwells within us in order to impart to us every good thing.

- To what end does the writer pray that God would equip His people with every good thing?

  The purpose of God's equipping believers with every good thing is so that He would enable us to do His will for His own good pleasure. God is working in His people to shape our desires, attitudes, and conduct in such a way that we will be able to do what is pleasing in His sight. Ultimately, God does all of this so that He will get the praise and the glory in Jesus Christ.

After the Video

- According to Dr. Charles, this benediction gives us three reasons why we ought to trust God for the help we need. What are those reasons?

  First, the benediction encourages us to trust God because He is the God of peace. Second, it instructs us to trust God because He is the God who raised Jesus from the dead. Finally, it teaches us to trust God for everything that we need because He has saved us forever through the blood of the everlasting covenant.

- From where does true peace come? How does John Blanchard define the phrase "the peace of God"?

  True peace comes from God alone. The writer of Hebrews calls God "the God of peace." He is the source of all true peace. God is the source, substance, and sustainer of peace. As Dr. Charles explained, "Where there is God, there is peace." John Blanchard defined the phrase "the peace of God" in the following way: "The peace of God is being grateful for past mercy, conscious of present mercy, and certain of future mercy."

- How ought the truth about God's raising Jesus from the dead affect our Christian lives?

  If God raised Jesus from the dead, He can work in us according to His power to meet any other need that we have. Whatever need we may have in life, it cannot take more of God's power than the power He worked in raising Jesus from the dead.

REVIEW QUIZ

Lesson 2

1. **C.**
   Though many Christians mistakenly believe that the saying "God helps those who help themselves" is biblical, Dr. Charles connected it to Benjamin Franklin, who made the saying popular. Scripture actually teaches that God helps those who are unable to help themselves. In Christ, He makes available all the strength, power, and help we need to be and to do all that He calls us to be and to do.

2. **C.**
   While the Gospels emphasize the fact of the resurrection, the Epistles highlight the significance of the resurrection. In this benediction in particular, we are taught that the resurrection of Jesus is proof that God is able to help us live in a way that is pleasing to Him.

3. **C.**
   Christians wrongly reduce the idea of peace to "negative realities"—namely, the absence of hostility, animosity and trouble. Instead, the biblical meaning of peace carries the idea of wholeness, completeness, blessing, and fulfillment.

4. **B.**
   The writer of Hebrews focuses on Jesus' role as our Great High Priest. When he speaks of the exaltation of Christ, he has in view his intercessory ministry on our behalf. Although he speaks of the resurrection of Jesus in only this one place in the letter, he assumes the truth of the resurrection when he speaks of the exaltation of Jesus.

5. **A.**
Dr. Charles explained that "everything good" refers to "the comprehensiveness of God's good gifts." He then listed the ordinary gifts of the Spirit, with which God equips all Christians, rather than the extraordinary gifts or other gifts for ministry. These are the gifts that enable us to live our lives in a way that is pleasing to God.

6. **C.**
God equips believers with every good thing so that they are able to do His will. This benediction does not speak of believers' finding out what God's will is for them. Neither does it teach that we will be able to do God's will in our own strength nor does it prompt us to inaction. Rather, it teaches us that God will sustain and equip us, by His grace, to do His will.

3

Preserved by God

INTRODUCTION

God calls His people to stand firm in the faith. But what are we to do when we recognize that we are unable to stand on our own? We must learn how to trust and praise God for preserving us by His grace. In this lesson, Dr. Charles draws our attention to Jude's closing doxology, explaining what it means that God is able to preserve us on earth and to present us to Himself in glory.

LEARNING GOALS

When you have finished this lesson, you should be able to:

- Identify the background of Jude's letter
- Explain the necessity we have to persevere in the faith
- Understand the relationship between our perseverance and God's preservation
- Recognize the reasons why God is worthy of our praise

KEY IDEAS

- God calls professing believers to persevere in the faith.
- God reassures His people that He is able to keep them from stumbling in the faith.
- The God who preserves believers is worthy of our exclusive, highest, and enduring praise.

REFLECTION & DISCUSSION QUESTIONS

Before the Video

What Do You Think?

Take a moment to answer the following questions. They will prepare you for the lecture.

- Have you ever given serious consideration to God's call for you to persevere in the faith? If so, what have you thought about your need to persevere?

Scripture Reading

Now to him who is able to keep you from stumbling and to present you blameless before the presence of his glory with great joy, to the only God, our Savior, through Jesus Christ our Lord, be glory, majesty, dominion, and authority, before all time and now and forever. Amen.

—Jude 24–25

- What does this passage teach us about the preserving grace of God?

During the Video

Answer the following questions while you watch the video. They will guide you through the lecture.

Trust the God Who Preserves *0:00–20:06*

- What assurance does Jude give his readers that God will keep them?

- Dr. Charles mentioned that all true Christians have experienced two miracles. What are they?

- How will God present us to Himself in glory?

Praise the God Who Preserves *20:06–25:56*

- Dr. Charles mentioned three kinds of praise of which God is worthy. What are they?

- What does the phrase "the only God, our Savior" teach us?

- How is the glory of God defined?

After the Video

Answer the following questions after you have finished the lecture. They will help you identify and summarize the major points.

- Why is it important to read Jude 21 in light of verse 24? What point did Dr. Charles make about the teaching of verse 24 at the beginning of this lesson?

  If you are in a group, have the members discuss the call for believers to persevere in the faith. Consider asking questions such as these: What does it mean for us to keep ourselves in the love of God? What are some ways that we can keep ourselves in the love of God?

- In this lesson, Dr. Charles distinguished between stumbling and falling. What is important about that distinction?

  If you are in a group, have the members discuss the encouragement they receive from this truth. Consider asking questions such as this: What does it mean that God is able to keep you from stumbling in your daily circumstances?

- According to Dr. Charles, what is the fuel of the Great Commission?

  If you are in a group, have the members discuss how this truth ought to impact the confidence we have in our witness and outreach for the sake of the gospel. Consider asking questions such as these: Have you ever been discouraged when you have witnessed to others? Do you sometimes forget that Christ has all authority in heaven and on earth and has promised to exercise it for the salvation of the elect?

PRAYER

Commit what you have learned from God's Word in this lesson to prayer.

- Praise God for His preserving grace.
- Confess your failure to recognize a daily need for God's power to preserve you.
- Thank God for giving you a renewed sense of His ability to keep you from stumbling.
- Ask God to give you a greater dependence on Him every day.

REVIEW QUIZ

Use these multiple-choice questions to measure what you learned from this lesson.

1. What is the purpose of the book of Jude?
   a. To comfort suffering believers
   b. To confront a compromising church
   c. To call believers to contend for the faith
   d. To encourage believers to love one another

2. When is God able to keep you?
   a. When you pray enough
   b. When you keep yourself
   c. When you cannot keep yourself
   d. When you try hard enough

3. Which attribute is in view when Jude says that God is able?
   a. Omnipresence
   b. Omnipotence
   c. Omniscience
   d. Oneness

4. According to Dr. Charles, to what does Jude refer when he speaks of God's keeping believers?
   a. Hardship
   b. Sickness
   c. Poverty
   d. Falling away

5. To what does the word "majesty" refer in verse 24?
   a. God's holiness
   b. God's mercy
   c. God's justice
   d. God's presence

6. What two words describe the way in which God has promised to present His people to Himself in glory in Jude 24?
   a. *Blameless* and *joyful*
   b. *Thankful* and *peaceful*
   c. *Humble* and *merciful*
   d. *Strong* and *courageous*

Answer Key—Preserved by God

REFLECTION & DISCUSSION QUESTIONS

Before the Video

What Do You Think?

These are personal questions. The answers should be based on your own knowledge and experience.

Scripture Reading

- What does this passage teach us about the preserving grace of God?

  Jude is calling us to see that we are dependent on our God and Savior to keep us from stumbling. From the beginning of the Christian life to the end, we need God's preserving grace because we cannot persevere in our own strength.

During the Video

Trust the God Who Preserves

- What assurance does Jude give his readers that God will keep them?

  Jude gives his readers the assurance that God will keep believers from stumbling by reminding them that God is able. God's perfect power is available to believers wherever they are, no matter what is happening in their lives. Jude is not giving his readers a remembrance of a time when God's power had worked in them. Neither is he speaking of a time in the future when God will work powerfully in the lives of His people. Rather, he is speaking of the fact that God is able to work in their lives at all times and in all circumstances.

- Dr. Charles mentioned that all true Christians have experienced two miracles. What are they?

  The first miracle that all true believers have experienced is the new birth. It is a miracle that God has brought us from spiritual death to spiritual life. The second miracle is that true believers are still saved. It is a miracle for anyone to continue to believe in Christ. The God who saves us is the God who keeps us.

- How will God present us to Himself in glory?

  God promises to present His people to Himself blameless and joyful. Left to ourselves, none of us is blameless. Only those who have been washed in the blood of the Lamb will be made to stand blameless on the day of judgment. Though Adam and Eve lost the joy of living in the presence of God when they sinned, Christ has taken away the guilt of our sin and removed the fear of judgment. We will rejoice in that day because we will stand clothed in His righteousness and will have been fully set free from sin. Additionally, God personally rejoices to bring us to Himself in glory. The writer of Hebrews tells us that "for the joy that was set before him" Jesus died to bring us to glory (12:2).

Praise the God Who Preserves

- Dr. Charles mentioned three kinds of praise of which God is worthy. What are they?

  God is worthy of exclusive praise, highest praise, and unending praise because He is the only God, and He is the God who keeps us. God is worthy of exclusive praise because He is the only God, our Savior. God is worthy of highest praise because He has all glory, majesty, dominion, and power. Finally, we are to give God unending praise because Christ is the same yesterday, today, and forever. The eternal God is the God who keeps us and presents us before the presence of His glory with great joy.

- What does the phrase "the only God, our Savior" teach us?

  Though the word Savior *in the New Testament usually has explicit reference to Jesus Christ, Jude's use of the term here is generally related to God as the One who preserves us. In this way, Jude is highlighting the fact that what Jesus has done, God has done.*

- How is the glory of God defined?

  According to Dr. Charles, we are to praise God for His glory, which is the sum total of all His attributes, the blinding light of His presence, and the crushing weight of His character.

After the Video

- Why is it important to read Jude 21 in light of verse 24? What point did Dr. Charles make about the teaching of verse 24 at the beginning of this lesson?

  True believers will persevere to the end because God is preserving them. They will not fall away from the faith because God will make them stand. God calls us to be steadfast in the faith and to keep ourselves in the love of God. However, verse 24 teaches us that God is able to keep us when we are unable to keep ourselves.

- In this lesson, Dr. Charles distinguished between stumbling and falling. What is important about that distinction?

  Stumbling precedes falling. Jude is not simply saying that God is able to restore people who have fallen. He is able to keep us from stumbling. Though the enemy is constantly seeking to trip believers up, God, as the psalmist declared in Psalm 121:3, "will not let your foot be moved."

- According to Dr. Charles, what is the fuel of the Great Commission?

  In the lesson, Dr. Charles explained that God's dominion is His manifest power at work in the world. In the Great Commission, Jesus said, "All authority in heaven and on earth has been given to me" (Matt. 28:18). The dominion of God in Christ is the fuel of the Great Commission.

REVIEW QUIZ

Lesson 3

1. **C.**

   The purpose of the book of Jude is to call believers "to contend for the faith that was once for all delivered to the saints" (v. 3). As false teachers were threatening the church, leading professing believers to turn away from the faith, Jude wrote to urge the remaining believers to stand fast in the truth.

2. **C.**

   Jude does not say that God is able to keep believers when they have prayed enough, tried hard enough, or served enough. Rather, he teaches that God is able to keep believers when they are unable to keep themselves. The preserving grace of God undergirds the perseverance of the saints—not the other way around.

3. **B.**

   God's ability is directly related to His omnipotence. As Dr. Charles noted, "To say that God is able is to say that He is omnipotent." It is not merely to say that He has good intentions. Rather, God will accomplish all that He intends to accomplish because He has power over all creation.

4. **D.**

   When Jude assures his readers that God is able to keep them, he is referring to God's keeping them from falling away from the faith. The context of Jude's letter demands that we understand this to be what he had in mind. Though many turn away from their profession of faith in Christ, Jude is assuring believers that God will keep them in the faith. Those who depart from the faith—as John tells us in 1 John 2:19—were never truly believers.

5. **D.**

   Though the word "majesty" is used in Hebrews 1:3 and 8:1 as a euphemism for God Himself, here it is used to denote God's presence. God is worthy of highest praise for His majestic power in the lives of His people.

6. **A.**

   Jude explains that God is able to present believers to Himself blameless and full of joy. Even though we are guilty and full of sin by nature, in Christ Jesus we will stand blameless before God—covered by His blood. In addition to removing the guilt of our sin in the death of Jesus, God has promised to fully remove the presence of our sin in glory. Where there is an absence of sin, there will be nothing but joy.

4

The Presence of God

INTRODUCTION

Each member of the Trinity is personally involved in the redemption of His people. In conferring spiritual blessings on believers, each of the three persons of the Trinity plays His respective role. In this lesson, Dr. Charles considers the Trinitarian benediction in 2 Corinthians 13:14 in order to stir up the hearts and minds of Christians to understand more of what blessings they have through God the Father, Son, and Holy Spirit.

LEARNING GOALS

When you have finished this lesson, you should be able to:

- Identify and describe each of the Trinitarian blessings contained in 2 Corinthians 13:14
- Know how each of these Trinitarian blessings applies to our lives

KEY IDEAS

- God's grace is His unmerited favor and undeserved kindness toward His people.
- By grace, believers have become the beneficiaries of all of God's blessings in Christ.
- After we have become recipients of God's grace in Christ, we experience the love of God.
- The Holy Spirit confers on us the blessing of fellowship with Himself and with other believers.

REFLECTION & DISCUSSION QUESTIONS

Before the Video

What Do You Think?

Take a moment to answer the following questions. They will prepare you for the lecture.

- Why would the Trinitarian nature of a benediction be significant?

- What role does the Holy Spirit play in the Christian life?

Scripture Reading

The grace of the Lord Jesus Christ and the love of God and the fellowship of the Holy Spirit be with you all.

—2 Corinthians 13:14

- What are the three blessings that come from the three members of the Trinity? What does this passage reveal about God's intention to bless His people?

During the Video

Answer the following questions while you watch the video. They will guide you through the lecture.

The Grace of Christ — *0:00–10:09*

- What is grace?

- What makes grace sufficient for the Christian's life?

The Love of the Father — *10:09–15:55*

- What does the order of this Trinitarian benediction reveal?

- What does Lamentations 3:22–23 teach us about God's love?

The Fellowship of the Spirit *15:55–24:11*

- Why have theologians sometimes called the Holy Spirit "the shy member of the Godhead"?

- Two kinds of fellowship are intended in the statement "the fellowship of the Holy Spirit." What are they?

After the Video

Answer the following questions after you have finished the lecture. They will help you identify and summarize the major points.

- What does God accomplish in the Christian's life by His grace?

  If you are in a group, have the members discuss the benefits of God's saving grace. Talk about why it is important for us to acknowledge the role that grace plays in each of the areas where Christ's redemption is applied to us.

- What story from the life of Charles Spurgeon was told in the lesson? What point was being made by use of this illustration?

  If you are in a group, have the members discuss how they view the love of God. Consider asking questions like these: Do you struggle to believe that God's love for you is unchangeable? Do you tend to measure God's love for you in light of your past failures or present circumstances?

- What account in the book of Acts was appealed to in order to prove that the Holy Spirit is a person and that He is God?

  If you are in a group, have the members discuss how they have typically viewed the Holy Spirit. Consider asking questions such as this: Are you tempted to focus on one person of the Trinity more than another?

PRAYER

Commit what you have learned from God's Word in this lesson to prayer.

- Praise each member of the Trinity for conferring spiritual blessings on you.
- Confess the ways in which you forget that all of the Christian life is by grace.
- Thank God for loving you with an unchanging, everlasting love.
- Ask God to strengthen you by the indwelling fellowship of the Holy Spirit.

REVIEW QUIZ

Use these multiple-choice questions to measure what you learned from this lesson.

1. What title has this benediction carried?
   a. "The Communion"
   b. "The Love"
   c. "The Grace"
   d. "The Fellowship"
2. What is the focus of this benediction?
   a. The triune God
   b. The ministry of Paul
   c. The blessings given to the church
   d. The perseverance of the saints
3. According to Dr. Charles, what is the purest expression of God's grace?
   a. His love
   b. His salvation
   c. His holiness
   d. His peace
4. What is indicated by the title "the Lord Jesus Christ"?
   a. The humanity of Christ
   b. The sovereignty of Christ
   c. The deity of Christ
   d. All of the above
5. In this lesson, Dr. Charles related several of God's attributes to His love. How did he relate God's grace to His love?
   a. Grace is God's forgiving love.
   b. Grace is God's overseeing love.
   c. Grace is God's proven love.
   d. Grace is God's restraining love.
6. To whom or to what is the Holy Spirit always telling people to look?
   a. The Father
   b. Himself
   c. The Son
   d. The church

Answer Key—The Presence of God

REFLECTION & DISCUSSION QUESTIONS

Before the Video

What Do You Think?

These are personal questions. The answers should be based on your own knowledge and experience.

Scripture Reading

- What are the three blessings that come from the three members of the Trinity? What does this passage reveal about God's intention to bless His people?

  The three blessings that come from the three members of the Trinity are grace, love, and fellowship. This passage reveals that all three members of the Trinity work together, according to each of their respective roles, to give assurance to believers.

During the Video

The Grace of Christ

- What is grace?

  Grace is God's unmerited favor to those who justly deserve God's judgment. It is the undeserved kindness and goodness of the One who is superior to us. Ultimately, grace is manifest in God's saving work in Jesus Christ.

- What makes grace sufficient for the Christian's life?

  Grace is sufficient for the Christian's life because the believer becomes the beneficiary of every spiritual blessing on account of it. This is precisely what the Apostle Paul emphasizes in Ephesians 1:3. Grace is also sufficient because the Lord Jesus Christ is its source. In this benediction, the Apostle gives it the title "the grace of our Lord Jesus Christ."

The Love of the Father

- What does the order of this Trinitarian benediction reveal?

  This benediction, though Trinitarian, is out of the typical order in which the members of the Trinity appear in Scripture. Ordinarily, the Trinity is spoken of in the following order: the Father, the Son, and the Holy Spirit. However, this is a declaration of praise to God for the redemption that we have in Christ. The benediction in 2 Corinthians 13:14 begins with the Lord Jesus Christ, because it is revealing that we cannot know the love of the Father until we know the grace of Christ.

- What does Lamentations 3:22–23 teach us about God's love?

  Dr. Charles explained, "God could never love you less than He loves you right now, and God can never love you more than He loves you right now." The application of this truth is that we don't have to worry about our past failures, and we don't have to be overwhelmed by our present circumstances.

The Fellowship of the Spirit

- Why have theologians sometimes called the Holy Spirit "the shy member of the Godhead"?

  The Holy Spirit has sometimes been called the shy member of the Godhead because He does not always appear beside the Father and the Son in certain places in Scripture. When He does appear, He is always pointing away from Himself and to the Son. The Apostle John recorded Jesus as saying that when the Holy Spirit comes, "he will glorify me" (John 16:14).

- Two kinds of fellowship are intended in the statement "the fellowship of the Holy Spirit." What are they?

  The first meaning is fellowship with the Spirit Himself. The second is fellowship with other believers through the Spirit. Regarding the direct fellowship of the Holy Spirit, He comes and indwells believers in order to assure them of the love God has for them in Christ. Respecting the fellowship of the Spirit in the communion with the saints, He binds us together in order to keep us united in Christian love.

After the Video

- What does God accomplish in the Christian's life by His grace?

  God accomplishes every aspect of the Christian's life by grace. We are chosen, called, justified, and sanctified by grace. We will also be glorified by grace. All of the Christian life is an ongoing work of grace.

- What story from the life of Charles Spurgeon was told in the lesson? What point was being made by use of this illustration?

  The story was told about Charles Spurgeon's looking at a weathervane that had the words "God is love" written on it. Spurgeon commented to a friend that this was the wrong sign for a weathervane because God's love is constant, whereas the weathervane moved with the wind. Spurgeon's friend responded in the following way: "Charles, I think you misunderstand the sign. The sign is meant to indicate, whatever way the wind blows, God is still love." No matter what storms may come, and no matter which way the wind blows in our lives, God's love for us is unchanging.

- What account in the book of Acts was appealed to in order to prove that the Holy Spirit is a person and that He is God?

  The account of Ananias and Sapphira in Acts 5 was appealed to in order to prove the personhood and divinity of the Holy Spirit. When Peter confronted them for their sin, he said, "Satan filled your heart to lie to the Holy Spirit. . . . You have not lied to man but to God" (vv. 3–4). Only a person can be lied to, and Peter equates the Holy Spirit to God.

REVIEW QUIZ

Lesson 4

1. **C.**
   Dr. Charles explained that this benediction has often carried the title "The Grace." It is one of the most well-known benedictions, commonly used by pastors to announce God's blessing on His people as they leave worship.

2. **C.**
   Though an initial consideration of this passage might lead some to conclude that it is about the triune God, the central focus of the passage is on the church and the blessings that the triune God confers on His people.

3. **B.**
   Grace includes every expression of God's undeserved kindness. However, God's salvation in Christ is the purest expression of His grace. Though we deserve God's condemnation and judgment, He has instead chosen to show us His favor in Christ.

4. **D.**
   The title "the Lord Jesus Christ" reveals the humanity, sovereignty, and deity of Christ. Every element in the title "the Lord Jesus Christ" represents a different aspect of His person. This ought to heighten our assurance of the pronouncement of blessing from Him.

5. **A.**
   Grace is God's forgiving love, and His love is at work in conjunction with all His other attributes. For instance, His mercy is His restraining love; His providence is His overseeing love; and His wisdom is His guiding love.

6. **C.**
   The Holy Spirit constantly tells people to look at Jesus. Jesus Himself explained this in John 15:26 when He said, "When the Helper comes, whom I will send to you from the Father, the Spirit of truth, who proceeds from the Father, he will bear witness about me." Again, in John 16:14, He said, "He will glorify me, for he will take what is mine and declare it to you."

5

Blessed by God

INTRODUCTION

The priestly benediction of Aaron is the great benediction of the Old Testament. In Numbers 6:22–27, the Lord commanded the priests to lift up their hands and pronounce this blessing over His people. By so doing, God affirmed His commitment to bless His people according to His will and by His Word. In this lesson, Dr. Charles considers the nature of this particular benediction and the fact that we can trust the God who pledged Himself to bless us.

LEARNING GOALS

When you have finished this lesson, you should be able to:

- Identify the specific blessings that God enumerates in the benediction in Numbers 6:22–27
- Understand that it is God who pronounces His blessing according to His own will
- Explain our reasons for trusting the God who pronounces His blessing

KEY IDEAS

- God is the source of all true spiritual blessing, which He confers on us according to His will.
- The blessings of God are all that we need in this life.
- Since God does not change, we can trust Him for all the spiritual blessings He has already secured for us and has promised to give to us.

REFLECTION & DISCUSSION QUESTIONS

Before the Video

What Do You Think?

Take a moment to answer the following questions. They will prepare you for the lecture.

- What do you think of when you ponder the blessings of God? What are God's best blessings?
- Do you struggle to believe that God wants to bless you?

Scripture Reading

The Lord spoke to Moses, saying, "Speak to Aaron and his sons, saying, Thus you shall bless the people of Israel: you shall say to them, The Lord bless you and keep you; the Lord make his face to shine upon you and be gracious to you; the Lord lift up his countenance upon you and give you peace. So, shall they put my name upon the people of Israel, and I will bless them."

—Numbers 6:22–27

- What is the essence of the benediction that God commanded the priest to pronounce over His people?

During the Video

Answer the following questions while you watch the video. They will guide you through the lecture.

The Blessings of God *0:00–10:39*

- How did the Old Testament priests decide to pronounce the blessing of God over the people?
- What is meant by the phrase "the disappearance of God"?

The God of Blessing *10:39–17:49*

- What biblical illustration is provided from 1 Chronicles in order to show that the blessings of God transcend the material blessings He gave Israel in the old covenant?

- What does it mean for God to make His face to shine upon us?

Trust the God of Blessing *17:49–23:08*

- How does God confirm His Word for His people?

- How does the grammar of the last verse in this benediction instruct us concerning the promise of future blessing from God?

After the Video

Answer the following questions after you have finished the lecture. They will help you identify and summarize the major points.

- What aspect of this benediction reveals that the blessings are about God rather than about us?

  If you are in a group, have the members discuss the importance of understanding the God-centered nature of His blessings. Consider asking questions such as this: What difference should it make to our prayer life when we consider that the Lord is the source and subject of all true spiritual blessing?

- Why is it important for Christians to recognize that the material blessings of God are meaningless apart from the spiritual blessing of God in Christ?

  If you are in a group, have the members discuss how we ought to view the material blessings God promised Israel in distinction from the spiritual blessings in the heavenly places spoken of in Ephesians 1:3.

- Why is it vital for us to understand that God not only plans and pronounces His blessing but also promises the fulfillment of it to His people?

If you are in a group, have the members discuss our need to be assured of the fulfillment of the promises of God. What are some reasons why we do not live as though we are assured of the promise of His blessing? What are some ways that we can grow in our confidence that He will do as He has spoken?

PRAYER

Commit what you have learned from God's Word in this lesson to prayer.

- Praise God for pronouncing His blessings over us.
- Confess your tendency to doubt the promises of God in Scripture.
- Thank God for putting His name on His people in order to confirm His promises.
- Ask God to help you see that He guarantees all His blessings to us in Christ.

REVIEW QUIZ

Use these multiple-choice questions to measure what you learned from this lesson.

1. With what New Testament prayer was this Old Testament benediction compared?
   a. Jesus' High Priestly Prayer in John 17
   b. The Lord's Prayer in Matthew 6
   c. The Apostle Paul's prayer in Ephesians 3:20–21
   d. "The Grace" in 2 Corinthians 13:14

2. What is the historical context in which this benediction appears in the book of Numbers?
   a. The Lord had just given Israel a major victory in battle.
   b. The priests were sacrificing in the tabernacle.
   c. God had given instruction concerning the Nazirite vow.
   d. God had made His first dwelling in the tabernacle.

3. What is *not* included in the blessings contained in Aaron's benediction?
   a. The blessing of peace
   b. The blessing of protection
   c. The blessing of health
   d. The blessing of God's presence

4. What meaning did Dr. Charles give for the Lord's lifting up His countenance upon us?
   a. That God is smiling on us in divine favor
   b. That God is overshadowing us with His protection
   c. That God is raining down His peace upon us
   d. That God is pleased with all that we have done

5. What does the name of a person represent in Scripture?
   a. His or her nature
   b. His or her character
   c. His or her authority
   d. All of the above

6. How can we be sure that we can trust the promises of God?
   a. Because we see the blessings in our lives
   b. Because we see the blessings in the lives of others
   c. Because we hear the blessings pronounced in church
   d. Because of the death and resurrection of Christ

Answer Key—Blessed by God

REFLECTION & DISCUSSION QUESTIONS

Before the Video

What Do You Think?

These are personal questions. The answers should be based on your own knowledge and experience.

Scripture Reading

- What is the essence of the benediction that God commanded the priest to pronounce over His people?

  This benediction contains pronouncements of the blessings that are the sum total of who God is and what He has promised to do for the spiritual good of His own. In this benediction, God vouchsafes His promised protection, provision, and presence to us.

During the Video

The Blessing of God

- How did the Old Testament priests decide to pronounce the blessing of God over the people?

  God commanded the priests to lift up their hands while pronouncing the precise words that God gave them in this benediction. God blesses according to His will and His Word. The Lord's name stands at the beginning of every line in the Aaronic benediction, indicating that He is the One who has determined to pronounce His blessing over His people.

- What is meant by the phrase "the disappearance of God"?

  In the opening books of the Old Testament, the Lord visibly appeared to His people. Then He began to establish His relationship with them primarily through His Word. The blessing of God is grounded on His Word. In this first blessing pronounced over His people, God did not give them something to see. He gave them a blessing to hear. In response, they were to take God at His Word.

The God of Blessing

- What biblical illustration is provided from 1 Chronicles in order to show that the blessings of God transcend the material blessings He gave Israel in the old covenant?

  After explaining that Israel would have understood the blessings in this benediction to include land and provision, Dr. Charles appealed to Jabez's request in

1 Chronicles 4:10. There, Jabez asked the Lord for material blessing—immediately after which he asked that God's hand would be with him. Dr. Charles explained, "The things of this world do not matter if you don't have God on your side."

- What does it mean for God to make His face to shine upon us?

  God doesn't have a body like those of people. The reference to God's face is an anthropomorphism—human terminology that expresses a divine reality in order to help our finite minds grasp the greatness of God. Scripture uses this language to represent the favor of God. The face of God is the favor of God that results in His being gracious to us.

Trust the God of Blessing

- How does God confirm His Word for His people?

  God puts His name on His people in order to confirm His Word. In Scripture, someone's name represented his or her person. The language suggests that God binds His character up in order to ensure the fulfillment of His promises. We have the undeserved favor, grace, and mercy of God because God puts His name on us.

- How does the grammar of the last verse in this benediction instruct us concerning the promise of future blessing from God?

  The grammar of the benediction in Numbers 6:24–26 conveys the idea that God is carrying out a habitual or ongoing act of blessing. However, in verse 27, the words "I will bless" intimate future blessing—a guarantee that God will provide for us in the future as He has done in the past. Dr. Charles explained, "You can live a long time on a promise if you trust the one who has made the promise."

After the Video

- What aspect of this benediction reveals that the blessings are about God rather than about us?

  The repetition of the Lord's name at the beginning of each pronouncement of blessing reveals that the blessings mentioned are about God and that He is the source and subject of all true blessing. In many respects, this benediction is the Old Testament counterpart to "The Grace" in 2 Corinthians 13:14.

- Why is it important for Christians to recognize that the material blessings of God are meaningless apart from the spiritual blessing of God in Christ?

  In Matthew 16:26, Jesus said to His disciples, "What will it profit a man if he gains the whole world and forfeits his soul?" Though the Israelites would have recognized a material element in the typical blessings of God in the old covenant, they also needed to recognize that material goods are meaningless apart from the God of spiritual blessings. Additionally, those who have been blessed by God with every spiritual blessing in the heavenly places are assured that God will keep them, no matter what attempts Satan or others may make to curse them.

- Why is it vital for us to understand that God not only plans and pronounces His blessing but also promises the fulfillment of it to His people?

  God is worthy of our trust because He does not change. God has promised to bless His people. In 2 Corinthians 1:20, the Apostle Paul explains that "all the promises of God find their Yes in him. That is why it is through him that we utter our Amen to God for his glory." God has fulfilled all His promises in the death and resurrection of Jesus. On account of the finished work of Christ, we are assured that we can trust all the blessed promises of God.

REVIEW QUIZ

Lesson 5

1. **B.**
   Dr. Charles suggested that the Aaronic benediction in Numbers 6:22–27 is comparable to the Lord's Prayer because it is universal in scope, never-ending in its efficacy, and always relevant for our needs. Though the Aaronic benediction was compared to what is known as "The Grace" in 2 Corinthians 13:14, that benediction should not be thought of as a prayer.

2. **C.**
   The context in which this benediction appears in the book of Numbers is quite unusual. It comes immediately after the regulations God gave for those who lived as Nazirites before Him. In following the very precise stipulations for the Nazirite lifestyle, those who adhered to it manifested that they were the recipients of God's blessings. However, immediately after the details surrounding the Nazirite vow, God commands the priest to pronounce His divine blessing over all His people.

3. **C.**
   Though the benediction of Numbers 6 is a pronouncement of blessing over the whole of a person's life, it does not promise a life free of physical suffering. The blessings enumerated would certainly have included material blessing in the old covenant era; however, they did so typically to point beyond material blessings to the higher and greater spiritual blessings that God confers on His people in Christ.

4. **A.**
   Dr. Charles said that the Lord's lifting His countenance upon us is equivalent to His "smiling on us in divine favor." It is an "expression of activity," in which His lifting His countenance upon us results in His giving us peace.

5. **D.**
   In Scripture, the name of a person represents his or her nature, character, and authority. It represents the whole of the person. When God says that He will put His name on His people, He is ratifying all His promises to them based on His nature, character, and authority.

6. **D.**
Ultimately, we can be sure that God has fulfilled and will fulfill all His promised blessings because Jesus has died for our sins on the cross and has been raised from the dead. When we fix our eyes on the crucified and risen Jesus, we are assured that God is faithful to His promises.

6

Sanctified by God

INTRODUCTION

God calls us as His people to pursue sanctification in the totality of our lives. Holiness is one of our greatest needs in the Christian life. However, we often fail to understand what part God plays in our sanctification. In this lesson, Dr. Charles breaks down the benediction in 1 Thessalonians 5:23–24 in order to stress the fact that our sanctification is built on the confidence that God is the One who sanctifies believers as we trust Him for this work of grace.

LEARNING GOALS

When you have finished this lesson, you should be able to:

- Explain God's role in the sanctification of believers
- Recognize our need to pray for sanctification
- List the reasons God gives us to trust Him for our sanctification

KEY IDEAS

- It is God's will and desire for believers to live sanctified lives.
- God has promised believers His sanctifying and preserving power and grace.
- God gives believers the strongest possible reasons why we should trust Him.

REFLECTION & DISCUSSION QUESTIONS

Before the Video

What Do You Think?

Take a moment to answer the following questions. They will prepare you for the lecture.

- Why ought we view sanctification as one of God's great blessings?

- Do you find in yourself a tendency to view sanctification as something entirely dependent on you? Or do you find in yourself an inclination to think that it is exclusively something God does in us?

Scripture Reading

Now may the God of peace himself sanctify you completely, and may your whole spirit and soul and body be kept blameless at the coming of our Lord Jesus Christ. He who calls you is faithful; he will surely do it.

—1 Thessalonians 5:23–24

- What does this passage reveal about the importance of the believer's sanctification?

During the Video

Answer the following questions while you watch the video. They will guide you through the lecture.

Asking God for Holiness *0:00–11:25*

- First Thessalonians 5:23–24 may be the least frequently used benediction in the writings of Paul. What explanation did Dr. Charles offer for why that may be the case?

- What two prayers does the Apostle Paul make on behalf of believers in 1 Thessalonians 5:23?

Trusting God for Holiness *11:25–25:33*

- In 1 Thessalonians 5:24, what three reasons Paul does give us for why we should trust God to sanctify and keep us?

- What does Paul have in mind when he speaks of the call of God? What does that call involve?

After the Video

Answer the following questions after you have finished the lecture. They will help you identify and summarize the major points.

- What was the illustration of a young man standing at Niagara Falls intended to convey?

  If you are in a group, have the members discuss the importance of knowing that we do not have the resources or ability in and of ourselves to accomplish the daunting task of producing holiness in our hearts and lives. Consider asking questions such as this: What are some of the ways that we deceive ourselves into thinking that our sanctification is attainable in our own strength?

- What does it mean for God to keep us blameless at the coming of the Lord Jesus Christ?

  If you are in a group, have the members discuss the distinction between sinless perfection and all-of-life obedience. Consider asking questions such as these: Do you find a propensity in yourself to grow careless about pursuing obedience and holiness? Why is it important for us to actively pursue holiness in every area of our lives?

- What assurance should we have that God will do that for which the Apostle prays in this benediction? How do we know that God will make believers holy?

  If you are in a group, have the members read Philippians 1:6 and have them discuss how it ought to stir up our confidence in the God of peace who promises to sanctify believers. Consider asking questions such as this: How should the truth of Philippians 1:6 affect our prayers to God for our sanctification?

PRAYER

Commit what you have learned from God's Word in this lesson to prayer.

- Praise God for giving us strong encouragement to ask and trust Him for holiness.
- Confess the ways in which we have not sought God to give us a greater measure of sanctification.
- Thank God for giving us a number of reasons to trust Him for a thorough sanctification of our lives.
- Ask God to increase His power in your life, increasingly conforming you into the image of Christ.

REVIEW QUIZ

Use these multiple-choice questions to measure what you learned from this lesson.

1. What title does God bear in 1 Thessalonians 5:23?
   a. The God of power
   b. The God of peace
   c. The God of hope
   d. The God of love
2. What did Dr. Charles refer to as "the undelegated work of God"?
   a. Redemption
   b. Justification
   c. Adoption
   d. Sanctification
3. What does the word *sanctify* mean?
   a. "To make faithful"
   b. "To make holy"
   c. "To make prayerful"
   d. "To make loving"
4. What term was inscribed on many ancient burial places of early Christians?
   a. "Without blame"
   b. "Holy to the Lord"
   c. "Redeemed"
   d. "Preserved"
5. Since God does the work of sanctification, believers "coast to glory."
   a. True
   b. False
6. What must we concentrate on if we are to grow in our trust in God?
   a. Our weakness
   b. Our Christian community
   c. God's faithfulness
   d. God's Word

Answer Key—Sanctified by God

REFLECTION & DISCUSSION QUESTIONS

Before the Video

What Do You Think?

These are personal questions. The answers should be based on your own knowledge and experience.

Scripture Reading

- What does this passage reveal about the importance of the believer's sanctification?

  This passage reveals that it is God's will that we would be sanctified in the whole of our being; it isn't merely a partial sanctification. Additionally, it teaches that God is committed to sanctify us as we prayerfully trust Him to do for us what we are unable to do for ourselves.

During the Video

Asking God for Holiness

- First Thessalonians 5:23–24 may be the least frequently used benediction in the writings of Paul. What explanation did Dr. Charles offer for why that may be the case?

  One possible reason why this benediction has been neglected is that we can become "so easily preoccupied with what we want *God to do for us that we neglect what we* need *God to do in us." Other benedictions speak of the goodness, favor, and blessings of God. This benediction speaks more directly about the internal reality of the believer's life.*

- What two prayers does the Apostle Paul make on behalf of believers in 1 Thessalonians 5:23?

  The Apostle Paul makes two petitions to God in 1 Thessalonians 5:23. First, he asks the God of peace to sanctify believers. Second, he prays that the God of peace would preserve those He sanctifies. Paul's prayer for the sanctification and preservation of believers is, in some sense, his asking for one and the same thing. Dr. Charles summarized these two requests in light of God's power to sanctify and preserve believers when he said, "God alone is able to clean us up, and God alone is able to keep us that way."

Trusting God for Holiness

- In 1 Thessalonians 5:24, what three reasons does Paul give us for why we should trust God to sanctify and keep us?

  Paul tells us that we can trust God to make us holy, sanctify us completely, and keep the entirety of our person because God has called us, God is faithful, and God has promised to do it. This is our great encouragement to trust God to do for us that which we cannot do for ourselves.

- What does Paul have in mind when he speaks of the call of God? What does that call involve?

  The call of God includes the external call of the gospel, the internal calling of God, and the ongoing call in the life of a Christian. The external call comes through the preaching of the gospel, by which God calls sinners to repent and believe. The internal call involves God's effectual calling of a sinner to Himself. The ongoing call involves the pursuit of holiness.

After the Video

- What was the illustration of a young man standing at Niagara Falls intended to convey?

  God doesn't delegate the work of sanctification. In this story, a young man who had just gotten his plumbing license was standing at Niagara Falls, saying, "I think I can fix this." The young man rashly thought that he could do what was impossible for him to do. In our sanctification, as Dr. Charles noted, "it is the will of God to have the Spirit of God use the Word of God to make the children of God look like the Son of God." Only the God of peace can do in us what we cannot do in ourselves.

- What does it mean for God to keep us blameless at the coming of the Lord Jesus Christ?

  The Apostle Paul is not teaching us that it is possible for a believer to attain to sinless perfection in this life. When he asks God to keep believers blameless until the day of Christ, he is asking God to give them a thorough obedience in which every aspect of their lives is consecrated to the lordship of Jesus. There can be no compartmentalization in obedience for the believer.

- What assurance should we have that God will do that for which the Apostle prays in this benediction? How do we know that God will make believers holy?

  Paul concludes his benediction by saying, "He will surely do it." There is no uncertainty in this declaration. Paul doesn't simply ask God to do it. The Apostle explains that God will surely *do it. In the words of Dr. Charles, "The caller is a doer." If God has begun a work in us, He will bring it to completion.*

REVIEW QUIZ

Lesson 6

1. **B.**
   The Apostle Paul opens this benediction by calling God "the God of peace." This title points to God's power, since He alone is able to keep the peace. It also represents God's enabling help. F.F. Bruce explained that the title "the God of peace" is representative of "the sum total of gospel blessings."

2. **D.**
   Though our redemption, justification, and adoption are all solely acts of God's grace, Dr. Charles called the sanctification of believers "the undelegated work of God." We are not able to resist temptation, live obediently, and fully submit to God on our own. Only God can make us what He calls us to be in Christ.

3. **B.**
   The word sanctify *means "to make holy." We are made positionally holy in Jesus Christ. We have also been redeemed by God to live a whole life of submission to Him and conformity to Christ. As we seek to do so, we begin to reflect the positional holiness that we already have in Christ. We have both been saved by grace and have been called to live our lives for God.*

4. **A.**
   Archaeologists have found burial places of early Christians that were marked with the phrase "without blame." He suggested that this was a reflection of the teaching of this benediction and of what God had promised to do for His people.

5. **B.**
   It is wrong for us to think that believers coast to glory because God has not delegated the work of sanctification to them. Christians are called by God to a high standard of following Christ. We are to be diligent in working out our own salvation, since God is working in us. This is the teaching of the Apostle Paul in Philippians 2:12–13.

6. **C.**
   If we are going to grow in our trust in God, we cannot focus on our own weakness. If doing so does not drive us to Christ, it can cause us to lose confidence. However, when we focus on the God who is faithful to bring about our sanctification, we grow in our confidence and trust in Him.

7

Strengthened by God

INTRODUCTION

Christians are called by God to endure hardship, suffering, and persecutions in this life. Though we are engaged in intense warfare with spiritual enemies, God gives us strong consolations and encouragements to strengthen us to stand in the grace of God. In this lesson, Dr. Charles considers the teaching of the benediction in 1 Peter 5:10–11, drawing out of it lessons about God's love and purpose for us in our suffering.

LEARNING GOALS

When you have finished this lesson, you should be able to:

- Explain the nature of the comfort that God gives believers in the midst of their suffering
- Describe the hope that believers have even when they suffer

KEY IDEAS

- The peace and love of God sustain believers during their suffering.
- God does not simply give believers saving grace; He gives them suffering grace.
- God puts a limit on the suffering of His people.
- The end of our suffering is the eternal glory of Christ.
- God wants us to learn from our suffering as He restores, confirms, strengthens, and establishes us.

REFLECTION & DISCUSSION QUESTIONS

Before the Video

What Do You Think?

Take a moment to answer the following questions. They will prepare you for the lecture.

- Have you ever been tempted to question whether God loved you during times of suffering or hardship?

- Do you see your inclination to long for a life free of hardship, suffering, or persecution?

Scripture Reading

After you have suffered a little while, the God of all grace, who has called you to his eternal glory in Christ, will himself restore, confirm, strengthen, and establish you. To him be the dominion forever and ever. Amen.

—1 Peter 5:10–11

- What does this passage reveal about God's plan and purpose for His people?

During the Video

Answer the following questions while you watch the video. They will guide you through the lecture.

Love in Suffering *0:00–12:33*

- For what reason was Peter writing this letter and this particular benediction to his readers? What was the historical background?

- To whom should we direct our fellow believers when they suffer?

- What contrast was made between what the enemy tells us and what we ought to conclude when we suffer?

Limit to Suffering *12:33–25:16*

- How does Peter express the fact that God puts a limit on the believer's suffering?

- According to this benediction, what is the ultimate end of our suffering?

- Why did Dr. Charles say, "God wants you to learn from your suffering"?

After the Video

Answer the following questions after you have finished the lecture. They will help you identify and summarize the major points.

- In the lesson, Dr. Charles explained that we sometimes misunderstand grace. What point was he making?

  If you are in a group, have the members discuss their own thoughts about God's grace. Consider asking questions such as these: Do you sometimes fall into this trap? Do you ever think that you have out-sinned the grace of God? If you do, what does that ultimately reveal about what you really believe about the grace of God?

- What do we need to remember about God's time frame when we suffer?

  If you are in a group, have the members discuss times when they wanted God to remove trials or sufferings sooner than He did. Encourage them to share personal examples.

- What two biblical illustrations were given to emphasize God's purpose to restore and confirm us after we suffer?

  If you are in a group, have the members read Luke 22:31–32 and 2 Corinthians 12:10. Consider asking questions such as this: What similar lessons has God taught us from our sufferings or trials? Encourage the members to consider times when they have looked back at their suffering and were able to see lessons that God was teaching them about His character.

PRAYER

Commit what you have learned from God's Word in this lesson to prayer.

- Praise God for His strengthening grace in times of suffering.

- Confess times when you have grown sinfully frustrated during times of suffering.
- Thank God for the assurance that He loves us when we are suffering.
- Ask God to keep your mind fixed on the fact that He has called you to His eternal glory in Christ.

REVIEW QUIZ

Use these multiple-choice questions to measure what you learned from this lesson.

1. This lesson explained the nature of the Christian life with a contrasting statement. What was it?
   a. "Christianity is a pilgrimage, not a vacation."
   b. "Christianity is a battleground, not a playground."
   c. "Christianity is a blessing, not a curse."
   d. "Christianity is a joy, not a burden."

2. What title did Peter ascribe to God at the beginning of his benediction?
   a. "The God of all glory"
   b. "The God of all praise"
   c. "The God of all grace"
   d. "The God of all peace"

3. According to Philippians 1:29, what is suffering?
   a. A judgment
   b. A gift
   c. A burden
   d. A grace

4. What does Peter say that God will do for you after you have suffered "a little while"?
   a. Fix your problems
   b. End your suffering
   c. Restore and confirm you
   d. Change your circumstances

5. In Matthew 7:24–27, Jesus teaches that the righteous are exempt from the storms of life.
   a. True
   b. False

6. What does the word "dominion" indicate in this benediction?
   a. God's presence
   b. God's dominance
   c. God's authority
   d. All of the above

Answer Key—Strengthened by God

REFLECTION & DISCUSSION QUESTIONS

Before the Video

What Do You Think?

These are personal questions. The answers should be based on your own knowledge and experience.

Scripture Reading

- What does this passage reveal about God's plan and purpose for His people?

  Peter encourages the suffering believers to whom he is writing to understand that God will not abandon them in the midst of their suffering. Rather, He who began a work of grace in their lives will sustain them and strengthen them during the time in which they are suffering in this life. God will ultimately give them eternal glory in Christ.

During the Video

Love in Suffering

- For what reason was Peter writing this letter and this particular benediction to his readers? What was the historical background?

  The Roman Empire was growing increasingly hostile to the Christian faith. As persecution was intensifying, Peter was writing to strengthen persecuted brethren with the knowledge of God's saving, sanctifying, and sustaining grace. He wanted them to be assured that God had a purpose for the suffering they were enduring.

- To whom should we direct our fellow believers when they suffer?

  We must point suffering believers to God because He has revealed Himself to us as the God of all grace. More than anything else, we need grace when we suffer. Peter doesn't simply call Him "the God of grace"—he calls Him "the God of all *grace." We need the assurance that we are united to the God of all grace and that we are to stand firm in this grace.*

- What contrast was made between what the enemy tells us and what we ought to conclude when we suffer?

  Though the enemy would have believers think that they are suffering because God doesn't love or care for them, the opposite is true. Peter wants us to know that no matter what we may be going through, we are the beneficiaries of the love and care of the God of all grace.

Limit to Suffering

- How does Peter express the fact that God puts a limit on the believer's suffering?

  In a brief statement that we might be tempted to pass over, Peter wrote, "After you have suffered a little while . . ." God reveals to us this principle that suffering has temporal limits so that we will know that He is the God of all grace and that He cares about us in the midst of our trials.

- According to this benediction, what is the ultimate end of our suffering?

  The end goal of our suffering is not our suffering; rather, it is eternal glory in Christ. Dr. Charles went on to illustrate this by relaying his tense and nervous experience when watching a television show or movie in which time seems to be running out for the person in distress or the hero. The key, he said, is to remember that the One who wrote the beginning wrote the end. In the same way, believers must remember that the One who wrote Genesis also wrote Revelation. Even though we suffer for a time, we have been called by God to eternal glory.

- Why did Dr. Charles say, "God wants you to learn from your suffering"?

  The word "restore" in this benediction is the same word used of the disciples' mending their nets in Matthew 4:21 and Mark 1:19. God will fix and perfect us through our suffering. One way He does this is by teaching us more about Himself as we suffer. Dr. Charles explained, "There are things about God I would not have learned . . . if I had not been afflicted."

After the Video

- In the lesson, Dr. Charles explained that we sometimes misunderstand grace. What point was he making?

  We sometimes mistakenly think that grace brings us into the family of God, but that if we mess up, He will kick us out. When we think in that way, we forget that the grace that saves us is the same grace that sustains us as sinners who have been made right with God.

- What do we need to remember about God's time frame when we suffer?

  God is not in a hurry. He does not work on our timetable. While it is frustrating to be stuck in a waiting room, it is more frustrating when our attitude is not right. The only thing that God tells us when we are in His sovereign waiting room is that the suffering will be only temporary.

- What two biblical illustrations were given to emphasize God's purpose to restore and confirm us after we suffer?

  The first illustration had to do with Simon Peter's fall and restoration. Jesus told Peter that He had prayed for him so that Peter would return to Him after Satan had sifted him. God's intended end was to restore and strengthen Peter for future ministry. The second illustration had to do with the Apostle Paul's thorn in the flesh. At first,

Paul prayed that the Lord would remove the thorn in the flesh. He then concluded: "I am content with weaknesses, insults, hardships, persecutions, and calamities. For when I am weak, then I am strong" (2 Cor. 12:10). Paul understood that God was both teaching him something about Himself and strengthening him through his suffering.

REVIEW QUIZ

Lesson 7

1. **B.**
   Dr. Charles made the statement "Christianity is a battleground, not a playground" in order to highlight the spiritual warfare in which believers are constantly engaged. First Peter 5:8 tells us that the devil walks about, seeking whom he may devour. He reveals this so that his readers would stand firm in the faith rather than run away in times of persecution.

2. **C.**
   Peter's benediction is the only place in Scripture in which God is described as "the God of all grace." It is important for us to consider the fact that Peter mentions this divine title to his readers in the context of their suffering, because we need grace more than anything else when we suffer.

3. **B.**
   For believers, suffering is a gift of God. The Apostle Paul explains this in Philippians 1:29 when he writes, "It has been granted to you that for the sake of Christ you should not only believe in him but also suffer for his sake." Suffering for Christ is just as much a gift from God as saving faith in Christ is.

4. **C.**
   Peter reminds his readers that God will restore and confirm them after they have suffered only "a little while." He doesn't tell them that He will change their circumstances, fix their problems, or end their suffering. Peter is teaching us that God has a reason why He allows us to suffer. As the psalmist declared in Psalm 119:71, "It is good for me that I was afflicted, that I might learn your statutes."

5. **B.**
   In Matthew 7:24–27, Jesus told the parable of the two houses built on different foundations. The foundations were tested by the storms that threatened the houses. Only the wise man who built his house on the firm foundation of the rock survived. In the same way, only those who stand on God's Word will be made firm when the storms of life come. The righteous are not exempt from the storms of life. Rather, they will have to endure them in this life.

6. **D.**
   At the close of his benediction, Peter gives God praise for His everlasting dominion. The word "dominion" carries the idea of God's presence, dominance, and authority. It is a reminder to suffering believers of God's manifest power. It is also a reminder that God is worthy of our praise even when we are suffering.

8

Glorying in God

INTRODUCTION

The New Testament doxologies are full of truths about God's character and glory. In this final lesson, Dr. Charles turns to the Apostle Paul's great doxology in Romans 11:33–36 in order to focus our attention on the surpassing greatness of God and the call for us to celebrate the wonder of His majesty.

LEARNING GOALS

When you have finished this lesson, you should be able to:

- Explain the importance of the structure of Paul's letters
- Identify the place of this doxology in the book of Romans
- Recognize the unsearchable greatness of God's wisdom and knowledge
- Understand the reasons why believers ought to celebrate God's greatness

KEY IDEAS

- The Christian life is framed by Apostolic teaching about Christian doctrine and duty.
- God's wisdom and knowledge are unsurpassably deep and insurmountably high.
- God does not receive counsel, and in all that we do give to God, He does not gain from it, since all things belong to Him.
- God is deserving of all praise because He is the ultimate source and end of all things.

REFLECTION & DISCUSSION QUESTIONS

Before the Video

What Do You Think?

Take a moment to answer the following questions. They will prepare you for the lecture.

- What are two major realizations that you have had during your study of these benedictions and doxologies from Scripture?
- Why do the authors of Scripture seem to break out in doxology when they write, even in the middle of a thought, argument, or letter?

Scripture Reading

Oh, the depth of the riches and wisdom and knowledge of God! How unsearchable are his judgments and how inscrutable his ways! "For who has known the mind of the Lord, or who has been his counselor?" "Or who has given a gift to him that he might be repaid?" For from him and through him and to him are all things. To him be glory forever. Amen.

—Romans 11:33–36

- What does this passage of Scripture teach us about God's greatness? How should we respond to the teaching of these verses?

During the Video

Answer the following questions while you watch the video. They will guide you through the lecture.

The Wonder of God's Greatness *0:00–12:01*

- What pattern does Paul use in structuring his letters in the New Testament? What does this structure teach us about Christianity?
- What two things does the Apostle Paul tell us about the greatness of God in Romans 11:33?

- What assurance do we gain from Paul's God-centered and God-exalting doxology?

The Truth of God's Greatness *12:01–24:57*

- What are two common ways in which we speak of God's attributes? How ought we to distinguish them?

- How does the truth about the unsearchable mind of God affect the way in which we approach others? In turn, what does our knowledge of others teach us about our inability to completely understand the mind of God?

- What is the first principle of Christian discipleship? How is this principle revealed in the life and teaching of King David?

After the Video

Answer the following questions after you have finished the lecture. They will help you identify and summarize the major points.

- At the beginning of this lesson, Dr. Charles warned about the danger of falling into one of two potential errors. What two errors must we seek to avoid?

  If you are in a group, have the members discuss the importance of considering whether a particular passage or section of Paul's letters is teaching doctrine or duty. Consider asking questions such as this: Do you ever examine yourself as to whether you are seeking to keep these two crucial aspects of the Christian faith together in your life?

- What do we learn about the counsel of God from the account of Job's interaction with God? How did Job approach God?

  If you are in a group, have the members read Job 38:1–5 and 42:2–6 together. Encourage the members to discuss what these passages of Scripture teach us about how we are to view God's sovereign counsel and will in regard to what He does in the world and in our lives. Ask them what Job's response teaches us about how we are to respond to God.

- What do we learn about the scope of God's greatness from Romans 11:36? What response should this truth elicit from us?

  If you are in a group, have the members discuss the significance of this teaching for our daily lives. If God is the source, sustainer, and significance of all things, how ought we to view our lives, relationships, and everyday circumstances?

PRAYER

Commit what you have learned from God's Word in this lesson to prayer.

- Praise God for revealing His unsearchable majesty in Scripture.
- Confess your failure to praise God daily for the depth of His riches, wisdom, and knowledge.
- Thank God for promising to give you wisdom as you daily recognize your need for it.
- Ask God to stir your heart to praise Him for the riches of His unsurpassable greatness.

REVIEW QUIZ

Use these multiple-choice questions to measure what you learned from this lesson.

1. Between what two things does Romans 11:33–36 serve as a bridge?
   a. Redemption and restoration
   b. Wisdom and knowledge
   c. Judgments and counsel
   d. Doctrine and duty
2. According to this doxology, with what is God rich?
   a. Power and glory
   b. Judgments and counsel
   c. Wisdom and knowledge
   d. Grace and mercy
3. What two things did Dr. Charles say that God doesn't need from you?
   a. Prayers and petitions
   b. Advice and assistance
   c. Adoration and affection
   d. Praise and thanksgiving
4. How did God respond to Job's demands for answers?
   a. God attempted to supplicate Job.
   b. God answered Job's deepest questions.
   c. God told Job to wait for answers.
   d. God questioned Job.

5. After we have looked into the truth of God's Word, what ought our response to be?
    a. Celebrate the wonders of God's greatness
    b. Embrace the truth of God's greatness
    c. Affirm the scope of God's greatness
    d. All of the above

6. What part of this doxology summarizes "the history of the world in one sentence"?
    a. "To him be glory forever."
    b. "Who has known the mind of the Lord . . ."
    c. "For from him and through him and to him are all things."
    d. "How unsearchable are His judgments . . ."

Answer Key—Glorying in God

REFLECTION & DISCUSSION QUESTIONS

Before the Video

What Do You Think?

These are personal questions. The answers should be based on your own knowledge and experience.

Scripture Reading

- What does this passage of Scripture teach us about God's greatness? How should we respond to the teaching of these verses?

  This passage teaches us that God's wisdom, knowledge, judgments, and ways are unsearchable. God doesn't need anything from us. He doesn't receive any counsel from us or from anyone else. No one can give anything to God. In light of the truth of His infinite greatness, the only thing left for us to do is to praise Him for His greatness.

During the Video

The Wonder of God's Greatness

- What pattern does Paul use in structuring his letters in the New Testament? What does this structure teach us about Christianity?

  In Romans—as in many of his other letters in the New Testament—the Apostle Paul first teaches the church doctrine and then exhorts the church to duty. These two aspects of Apostolic revelation must always remain together in the Christian life. They ought never to be separated. As Dr. Charles explained, "Christianity is not to be religious activism devoid of theological understanding. At the same time, it's not to be intellectual assent devoid of personal devotion." Paul's doxology in Romans 11:33–36 serves as a bridge between doctrine and duty.

- What two things does the Apostle Paul tell us about the greatness of God in Romans 11:33?

  The Apostle Paul, not simply making an intellectual statement, exclaims with heartfelt wonder that the greatness of God is too deep for us to understand and too high for us to comprehend.

- What assurance do we gain from Paul's God-centered and God-exalting doxology?

  The Apostle Paul teaches us to celebrate the wonders of God's greatness, even when we do not understand what God is doing, because we have the assurance that God—in His greatness—knows exactly what He is doing.

The Truth of God's Greatness

- What are two common ways in which we speak of God's attributes? How ought we to distinguish them?

  Theologians have commonly spoken of God's communicable and incommunicable attributes. The communicable attributes of God are His characteristics that we can emulate. For instance, God shares wisdom and knowledge with us. By way of contrast, God's incommunicable attributes are those perfections of God that are beyond our comprehension or ability to emulate. When Paul speaks of the infinite and eternal counsel of God in this doxology, he is referring to God's incommunicable attributes.

- How does the truth about the unsearchable mind of God affect the way in which we approach others? In turn, what does our knowledge of others teach us about our inability to completely understand the mind of God?

  We can think God's thoughts after Him only insofar as He has revealed them to us in His Word. This means that we should deal carefully with one another. We should resist the urge to criticize the motives of others because we do not know what is in their hearts—after all, we do not even know what is in our own hearts. If we do not know the depths of the depravity of our own hearts, how can we possibly know the mind of God? Our inability to know ourselves completely or judge the motives of others further shows us that we cannot completely know the mind of God.

- What is the first principle of Christian discipleship? How is this principle revealed in the life and teaching of King David?

  The first principle of Christian discipleship can be stated in four words: "God owns it all." We cannot give God anything. Anything that we give Him already belongs to Him. David, in Psalm 24:1, declares, "The earth is the LORD's and the fullness thereof, the world and those who dwell therein." Though David's desire was to build the temple for God, God would not allow him to do so, but God did allow David's son, Solomon, to build it. After receiving the gifts of the people of Israel for its future construction, David prayed: "But who am I, and what is my people, that we should be able thus to offer willingly? For all things come from you, and of your own have we given you" (1 Chron. 29:14).

After the Video

- At the beginning of this lesson, Dr. Charles warned about the danger of falling into one of two potential errors. What are two errors must we seek to avoid?

  Paul's letters follow the pattern of teaching about doctrine to teaching about duty. All of the Christian life is built on the divinely inspired teaching about belief and behavior. We must guard against the error of embracing an unthinking devotion, and we must seek to avoid the error of embracing uncommitted doctrine. God intends the teaching of the faith and teaching about the life of faith to remain together.

- What do we learn about the counsel of God from the account of Job's interaction with God? How did Job approach God?

  The account of Job reveals that no one can be God's counselor. Job came to God in the midst of his suffering with questions about God's moral government. He demanded that God answer his questions. When God finally appeared, He did not come to answer Job's questions; rather, He came to question Job. In this way, God taught Job that He will do whatever He wishes and that no one will give Him counsel.

- What do we learn about the scope of God's greatness from Romans 11:36? What response should this truth elicit from us?

  In Romans 11:36, the Apostle Paul summarizes the scope of God's greatness by telling us that all things are from God, through God, and to God. He is the source, sustainer, and significance of all things. All things originate in Him, are preserved by Him, and are terminated by Him. He is the beginning and the end of all things. In light of this truth, we are left with nothing but to praise Him. Paul follows his statement of the scope of God's greatness with the declaration, "To him be glory forever."

REVIEW QUIZ

Lesson 8

1. **D.**
   The doxology in Romans 11:33–36 serves as a bridge between Paul's teaching about Christian doctrine in the first part of Romans and his teaching about Christian duty in the second part of Romans. Paul does not move from doctrine to duty without stopping to rejoice and to praise God for the glory of the truth of the doctrine He has just revealed to His church.

2. **C.**
   According to this doxology, God is rich in wisdom and knowledge. Paul tells us that God's riches are deep. He then tells us that God's riches are deep in wisdom and knowledge. Dr. Charles explained that wisdom and knowledge belong side by side; as his former pastor used to state, "Wisdom teaches knowledge how to behave."

3. **B.**
   Dr. Charles explained that this doxology reveals that God doesn't need your advice or assistance. God doesn't need our advice because He is unsearchable in His greatness. None of us can know the infinite greatness of the mind of God. None of us teach God anything. God doesn't need our assistance because we can give God nothing that isn't already His. Whatever we have, whatever we are, and whatever we do all have God as their source.

4. **D.**
   In the midst of his suffering, Job demanded answers from God. He asked God to explain his suffering. When God finally addressed Job, He refused to answer his questions. Rather, God questioned Job: "Where were you when I laid the foundation of the earth?" (Job 38:4). In turn, Job finally came to acknowledge his inability to advise or assist God (42:2–6).

5. **D.**
   After we have looked into the truth of God's Word, we must look up to God in worship—celebrating the wonders of His greatness, embracing the truth of His greatness, and affirming the scope of His greatness.

6. **C.**
   According to Dr. Charles, Romans 11:36 contains the history of the world in one sentence—namely, "For from him and through him and to him are all things." God is first, efficient, and final cause of all things. No matter who you are or what your story is, the testimony of your salvation is summed up in this one statement.